D1542247

VIOLA DAVIS

Table of Contents

Chapter 1

Farm Shack to White House

In a frank and intimate conversation in their pre-presidency home—a Georgian revival mansion on Greenwood Avenue in the Kenwood neighborhood of Chicago, Illinois—Michelle and Barack Obama discuss the dangers of his running for president. Michelle is wearing a creamy off-white blouse and necklace of pearls, and everything about her—her voice, her stance, the way she contorts her face—shows that she is not happy. Meanwhile, Barack takes on a more relaxed stance, more exasperated than angry, as he crosses his arms before himself and listens to his wife.

Michelle's point? Because Barak is black, he'll be in more danger as a candidate than others. He'll need more Secret Service protection, and he'll need it earlier than any other candidate before him.

Barack responds with tired confusion. "Just.... I could be President of the United States," he says, raising a hand to interrupt his wife. "Could you find it in yourself to be a little excited for me?"

"Excuse me if I can't share in the excitement of my husband potentially being shot."

It's a powerful moment, and it shows the fear and drama the Obama family was feeling prior to Obama's presidency, a fear all presidential families share but—to Michelle's point—a fear that is greater for the Obama family because of race. The scene is powerful and thought-provoking. But it isn't actually Michelle and Barak that we see. Instead, the scene is played by O-T Fagbenle as Barack and Viola Davis as Michelle, part of the first episode of Showtime's limited series *The First Lady*.

Viola Davis has played numerous characters in her career on the stage and on both TV and movie screens. She's played a wife and mother in *Fences*, a housemaid in *The Help*, and the comic-book character Amanda Waller in *Suicide Squad*. But playing Michelle Obama was one of her most challenging roles to date for two reasons. First, she's a personal friend of the First

Lady. Second, she played a recent and well-loved public figure. Playing someone famous that people still remember is very different from playing a distant historical figure. And yet, even though there was some inevitable criticism regarding her portrayal of the famous Mrs. Obama, most fans have sung praises for her courage and daring creative choices.

From Humble Beginnings to The First Lady

It has been a long road for Viola to get to play one of the most popular and culturally influential women of our time. She started with some of the humblest beginning imaginable—being born in a one-room shack in the mid-sixties south—growing up angry at the world and lacking an outlet for her creative and passionate energies. But acting soon became her outlet, and she funneled every ounce of emotion into the stage and camera, and that passion has since paid off in a big way.

When viewers think of Viola Davis, they may think of Michelle Obama in the Showtime series *The First Lady*, but they might not. Fans of the TV series *How to Get Away with Murder* will know her from that. Comic book fans will know her as Amanda Waller. Even those that do not know her from her many film and TV roles may know her from her association with Oprah, her philanthropic work, or her memoir. Finally, parents may know her as the author of the sequel book to the children's classic *Corduroy*.

However you might know Viola Davis, one thread stitches throughout all of her work: her passion and intensity on the screen. She does not play weak or mild women. She does not play roles that slip into the background on the stage or screen. Instead, she consistently plays characters that are larger than life, intense, and headstrong. Her parts, no matter how minor, consistently steal the show, becoming dramatic highlights of the narrative. As a result, even when the movie or play in question is met with poor or mixed reviews, even when critics near-universally bomb the story or acting or direction, they almost always save a few editorial inches to set Viola apart as one of the few redeeming qualities of the piece.

So how has the long and bumpy road taken shape over the years, this trek from poor girl from a large family to a TV and film star? This book will trace Viola's life and career, painting a picture of her rise to stardom through practice and passion.

In the following two chapters, we'll look at her family life growing up, her school years, and her eventual stay in one of the top acting schools in the country. Then, starting in Chapter 4, we'll look at Viola's career as an actress, starting with her earliest roles to her first breakout parts. After a brief stop-off to talk about her family as an adult, we'll dive back in to see the awards she accrued over the years and some of the parts she's most known for.

In Chapter 9, we'll look at one of the roles that has shaped her career, her TV career on *How to Get Away with Murder*. Finally, we'll look at the role we discussed at the outset, that of playing Michelle Obama on Showtime. We'll see that, while some have criticized some of her acting decisions, she has also earned the respect and admiration of many fans for her bold choices and dedication to her portrayal of one of the most beloved women to ever live in the White House.

Finally, we'll talk about her books and ongoing relationship with Oprah, as well as the work she's done to help children growing up now in circumstances not much different from those Viola endured herself as a young girl.

Through all of this, a picture emerges, the portrait of a woman who has worked tirelessly to bring drama and emotion to the screen, a woman who didn't listen when others criticized her or predicted she would fail. Instead, she threw herself into her work in the only way she knew how—with an intense passion and love for the art form. Viola is a master at her craft, and what follows is her story.

Chapter 2

Humble Beginnings

It was warm, dry, and windy in August of 1965 in the area around St. Matthew's Township, North Carolina. For the pregnant Mary Alice Davis, the 89-degree afternoons were a blessing compared to the 100-plus-degree summer they'd just endured. And yet, as the contractions came, she wished it were cooler. Wouldn't some rain cool things down a bit? Sure, but it was unusually dry that month, and as the contractions got closer and closer to one another, Mary Alice—who had already given birth to four children before this one, knew exactly what to expect.

This labor did not happen in a hospital or even in a comfortable room in a house. There were no doctors or nurses on hand. Instead, they were in the one-room shack on Mary Alice's mother's sharecropper's farm. Her mother was the only other person there with her, walking her through the waves of pain and calm moments between them. Finally, after hours of labor, a baby girl was brought into the world, crying and screaming and demanding to be loved. Mary Alice and her husband Dan Davis would name the baby girl Viola.

This was how Viola Davis came into the world, into a poor black family in the South, in the middle of a sharecropper's farm - a farm that was once a plantation. And yet, despite all of these disadvantages and constant reminders of the injustice of American life, she was loved and cared for. Her headstrong attitude would get her into trouble from time to time as a young girl, but she would eventually channel that energy into something remarkable—acting.

From North Carolina to Rhode Island

Viola came from some of the humblest of beginnings. Her father, Dan, was a horse trainer, and her mother, Mary Alice, was a housemaid and a factory worker. A couple of months after being born, Viola and her parents moved from North Carolina to Central Falls, Rhode Island. Two of her older siblings went with Viola and her parents. Her oldest brother and sister would stay behind with the grandparents.

Many times, poor rural families move to the city with the hope of finding a better life, of getting good work, and moving the children into a nice apartment. The reality, though, for many, is very much the opposite. In the case of the Davis family, they moved into an abandoned building that was eventually going to be torn down. However, in the meantime, they were allowed to live there.

Viola recalls not being able to sleep at night because of the rats that lived in the buildings she slept in. They could hear the rats above them, killing the pigeons in the attic space, scurrying about in the walls. The thought of a vicious rat nearly the size of a cat hunting and killing other creatures was terrifying for a tiny Viola.

Many years later, Viola would describe her life as a child as "abject poverty." She told the Wall Street Journal once, "I was a kid who was hungry. I grew up in abject poverty. I dumpster-dived. I stole money for food."

Her mother was involved in the Civil Rights Movement, and Viola even went to jail with her mother at the age of 2 because they'd been arrested in a protest. Viola also recalls, as a young girl, walking to the local branch of the public library every day to read books, a habit solidified by a friendly librarian who would share her lunch with Viola every day.

Viola's School Years

As a young student, Viola was often in detention, not because she was a bad kid, but because the hunger and poverty she had experienced her whole life made her angry and distracted. Poverty was a significant problem in the area where she lived, and yet, in a family of 6 children, Viola was poorer than most, and that felt very unfair for a young child.

She would go on to attend Central Falls High School, a place that, many years later, would be rated as one of the worst schools in the entire state and would have to reform in harmony with federal law.

Teenaged Viola Davis needed direction in her life. She needed an outlet for the anger and passion she felt. Thankfully, an unexpected role model would inspire her toward a particular outlet that would shape the rest of her life—acting.

The Moment that Changed her Life

The Autobiography of Miss Jane Pittman was a film released in 1974, starring Cicely Tyson, an actress of color, in the leading role. When a young Viola saw that film, she instantly fell in love with acting. Tyson was fantastic in the film, and it was the first time Viola had seen a black woman take charge in a creative art. A new road of opportunity was now open for Viola, and it was a road she was excited to explore.

She began taking art and theater classes in school, anything that could get her closer to her new dream. Later, Viola would enroll in the Young People's School for the Performing Arts in West Warwick, Rhode Island. There, Bernard Masterson, a director in the program, quickly saw her talent and encouraged her to continue.

After she graduated from high school, Davis went on to study at Rhode Island College, where she majored in theater. She would also participate in the National Student Exchange. She graduated in 1988, but her schooling would not end there. She would go on to study in one of the most prestigious schools for actors in the country—Juilliard.

Chapter 3

Juilliard

Take a walk along Broadway in Downtown New York City, smelling the smells of food carts spaced along the sidewalk, first hot dogs, then Greek street kebobs, then hoagies with steaming sauerkraut and stone-ground mustard. Pick the right time of day for your walk, and there won't be too much traffic on the street or the sidewalk, and you'll enjoy the shade of the trees planted along the side of the street.

Around the corner, up on West 65th Street, there's the famous Lincoln Center of the Performing Arts, complete with an upscale restaurant, multiple theaters, and a park area for visitors. But, before we reach that corner on Broadway, you'll notice a little amphitheater just off the sidewalk under the shadow of an angular building. Hot dog in hand, take a seat there on the cool concrete bleachers and look up.

Protruding from the side of the building is what looks like a squat glass box. Inside the box—if you're lucky—you'll see dancers moving and twisting, gyrating to music you can't hear but can imagine as you watch the rhythm of their bodies. You sit back and enjoy the show. That's what it is, after all, a show. Why else would they be in a room that hangs out from the rest of the building, a room of all-glass walls, as if on display?

The room you're looking up at? A dance studio for only the most serious and talented of young dancers. The building you rest in the shadow of? Juilliard School of Music.

Let us take a moment to talk about the school that Viola Davis went to on scholarship. Then, while we're at it, let us see what Viola had to say about her time there all those years ago.

The History of Juilliard

Juilliard has a long and rich history in New York City, starting as the Institute of Musical Art in 1905. The idea behind the school was simple. Too many students were going off to Europe to study music because no American school of fine arts could compete with those across the seas. Later, when a wealthy businessman named Augustus Juilliard died, he left a large sum of money to the school to aid in the development of the musical arts, something he had enjoyed his entire life. As a result, the school was renamed the Juilliard School of Music.

Many people still commonly call the school by that name, which is fitting because music is the most prominent focus of the institution. That being said, the name was officially changed to Juilliard School in 1968 to reflect a broadening of its core mission to include instructing directors, actors, and dancers in addition to musicians.

Juilliard Today

Today, the beautiful campus of Juilliard school sits along Broadway, as was described above. It trains some of the greatest musicians, composers, dancers, choreographers, directors, actors, and screenwriters in the country.

In 2015, it was announced that Juilliard would open its first major branch outside the US, a school in Tianjin, China. The school was officially opened in 2020 and offers a Master of Music degree program for a limited number of students.

Viola Davis—Young Theater Student

Viola learned a great deal from her teachers and fellow students at Juilliard. And yet, at the same time, she experienced some degree of racism in the school, too. She'd later describe it this way:

"That was my issue with Juilliard. Whatever character I play, I'm not gonna play with the same palette as my white counterparts because I'm different. My voice is different. Who I am is different? It was like, 'Your voice is too deep, you're too hard. So, you have to be light, but you have to be light like a 90-pound white girl. You can't be your light.'"

Even in a progressive and creative place like Juilliard, Viola had to deal with racial pressures, a constant reminder that she wouldn't be considered "pretty" enough for some roles, or "too hard, too deep." When all these things would really be like code for "too black."

Despite this, she graduated from Juilliard, ready to take on the world as a young actress.

Chapter 4

On the Stage and in TV

On a starship far from Earth, a mystery unfolds in the movie *Solaris*, a mystery that involves love, identity, manipulation, and what it means to be human. While this movie stars George Clooney and Natascha McElhone, this eerie art film also features an appearance from Viola Davis, who plays the guarded and traumatized Dr. Gordon.

In Davis's most memorable scene of the movie, Dr. Gordon talks to Clooney's Dr. Chris Kelvin. "We're in a situation that is beyond morality," Gordon says, talking about the mysterious happenings as the ship orbits the planet Solaris.

Gordon is cold and guarded. Her stony expression is amplified by her gray attire, which, in turn, is supported by the gray metal and glass background. The normally reserved doctor explodes with emotion at Kelvin. "She's a copy… a facsimile, and she's seducing you all over again." Her eyes stare with intense disgust. "You're sick."

In this scene, among others, Viola showcased her acting skills to an audience that still didn't know her at all, especially since this was her meatiest film role to date. And yet, as *Solaris* was released in 2002, Viola was already on the rise as a talented and passionate actress on both the stage and the screen. So let us look at her early career after graduating from Juilliard and see how she came to be poised to rise to stardom in the early 2000's.

Early Stage Appearances

In the early and mid-1990s, Viola was able to star in various professional and off-Broadway plays. For example, in 1992, she played Denis in *As You Like It,* a comedic play written by none other than William Shakespeare. By 1996, she had made it to Broadway, playing as Vera in August Wilson's play *Seven Guitars*.

While reviewers would not yet single out viola's roles, as would be the case later in films such as *Doubt,* many of the plays she had roles in did very well and received excellent reviews.

Later, in the 2000's she would continue to appear in numerous plays, such as King Hedley II, in which she won her first Tony for best actress.

TV Roles

Around the same time, Viola was picking up minor roles in some of the major TV series of the time. In 1996, she played small parts in *NYPD Blue*, *New York Undercover*, and *The Pentagon Wars*. In 1999, she appeared in a comedy film called *Out of Sight*. Her TV and stage appearances would lead to small roles in films, which we'll highlight next.

Early Film Success

Viola would play in several films in the early 2000s, although none of the roles would be major or particularly highlighted by critics. She appeared in *Traffic* and the above-mentioned sci-fi film, *Solaris*. In 2005, she played in George Clooney's movie *Syriana*. Many of these films were due to her ongoing working relationship with Steven Soderbergh.

Davis would also have a short scene in *Ocean's Eleven and* the romantic comedy *Kate & Leopold*.

In the 2002 film *Antwone Fisher*, Viola played the boy's mother, who is absent for almost all of the movie. She has a small appearance in the beginning and once again toward the end. This was a significant role for Viola, even though she had very few lines in the film. Because the whole movie - and the main character's psyche - hinged on his relationship with his mother, she was a significant character in the movie despite the short screen time. Viola would pull off the role exceptionally well, perhaps laying the groundwork for *Doubt*, in which another very small role would earn Viola much attention and eventually an Oscar nomination.

Chapter 5

Starting a Family

A young actress living in Los Angeles, Viola started to get her first taste of big-time success. But there was one thing missing in her life, something she desperately wanted—a steady romantic relationship. But looking for a husband in the Hollywood scene can be loaded with headaches and heartache, and she wanted none of that. In the end, however, she found someone she could truly be happy with. And it all started with him walking up and giving her his business card.

"He had a shirt on," Viola recollects—something that was not common among young male actors she'd met. That stood out to her. It meant, perhaps, that he was a man with class. Marriage material? Viola knew of only one way to find out.

Here is the story of Viola's marriage to Julius Tennon, a story that starts with, of all things, a prayer. This love story also includes doubts and depression, and struggle. Nevertheless, it's also a story with a happy ending—something incredibly rare in the world of showbiz.

Praying for a Husband

While living alone in LA, Viola wanted a husband. A friend of hers suggested that she pray for the kind of man she wanted, and that's exactly what she did. She would later recall getting on her knees and praying for the man who would become her husband.

"I said I want a big Black man from the South who's probably been married before, has kids, because I don't want any pressure in that department." Quite the specific prayer! "Three and a half weeks later, I met Julius from Texas. Ex-football player, been married, raised his children on his own, was an actor."

It seemed like a dream come true, except that Viola didn't get back in touch with Julius. Why not?

"What Do I Have to Offer?"

Julius later described the situation as perfect for him, as well. He was in the middle of a relationship that wasn't great, and he needed someone different. So when he met Viola at an event and overheard that she was single and looking for a relationship, he immediately introduced himself and gave her his card.

Viola waited weeks before finally calling him. Why? Because she didn't think she had anything to offer him. She was a poor actress with lousy credit. Eventually, her friends convinced her to give things a try, reminding her that she had prayed for someone just like him. When she did reach out to Julius, he invited her to church. That sealed the deal for her.

Twenty Years Later
Viola and Julius were married in 2003. They would later have a baby girl together, naming her Genesis. Years later, she and Julius still appear together at awards shows and in interviews, actively supporting one another through life and careers. All because she followed some advice to pray for the man she wanted!

Chapter 6

Doubt

A black-shrouded nun named Sister Aloysius Beauvier, who is also the principal of a Bronx parish school, walks, huddled against the cold, swaddling an old, hand-carved umbrella. Her face is pale against the black of her bonnet, and thin, wire-framed glasses sit perched on the bridge of her nose. She walks alongside a middle-aged black woman, also bundled up in the cold and holding onto a much plainer umbrella of her own.

The sister is trying to discuss a sensitive topic with the woman—her young son who attends the parish school, a boy named Donald Miller. Donald just so happens to be the only black boy attending the school, and the mother wants nothing more than for him to graduate from the school. Graduation, Mrs. Miller explains, would mean Donald can get into a good high school, which, in turn, means he'll have a better chance at college.

Sister Aloysius is concerned, however, about suspicions she has come to have regarding Father Brendan Flynn, a priest serving at the parish school's Catholic church. She believes Father Flynn has made sexual advances toward the boy. She expresses her suspicions, expecting Mrs. Miller to be outraged. The mixed emotions on the mother's face, however, tell a much deeper and more nuanced story.

"I don't think you completely understand," the sister says.

"I understand the kind of thing you're talking about, but I don't want to get into it," the mother responds, shocking Aloysius with her seemingly callous attitude. But, as the conversation develops, it becomes clear that this boy's mother is willing to look past anything, even possible molestation, if it means her son gets a chance at the future she wants for him. More than that, she hints that exposing the situation could incur the wrath of the boy's father. In fact, it could lead to the boy's death.

This shocking scene from the 2008 film *Doubt* lasts a little more than 7 minutes. The mother, played by Viola Davis, has only this small scene in the movie. The Sister is played by Meryl Streep, a powerhouse of dramatic acting in her own right. In fact, *Doubt* is a movie, now over a decade and a half old, known for its outstanding acting. Yet, critics at the time didn't only praise the leading actors and actresses in the landmark film. They also took some time to praise Viola for her short but powerful contribution, a small scene that brought power to the entire narrative, a part that led to her receiving an Oscar nomination.

Praise for Doubt—and Viola

Doubt was immediately recognized as a fantastic movie. On Rotten Tomatoes, we read the consensus: "*Doubt* succeeds on the strength of its top-notch cast, who successfully guide the film through the occasional narrative lull."

This is a movie that is universally praised for its excellent acting. While the leading roles were praised by critics—and for very good reason; we see Meryl Streep in one of her best performances here—Viola Davis also got many mentions even though she only appears in the movie for a little over 7 minutes.

One review described Viola's performance as "a near-miraculous level of believability" The review continued: "Davis, in her small, one-scene role, is incredibly moving—I can barely remember a Davis performance where I haven't been moved ... [she] plays her character, an anxious, hardworking woman who's just trying to hold her life and family together, by holding everything close. She's not a fountain of emotion, dispensing broad expression or movement; instead, she keeps it all inside and lets us in".

It's of little surprise, then, that she was nominated for multiple awards because of the role, including her first Oscar nomination.

The Academy

Speaking of the Oscars, it was a year later, in 2009, that Davis was inducted into the Academy of Motion Picture Arts and Sciences. She would go on to receive more nominations in the future, and she'd eventually win an Academy Award for her role in Fences, which we will talk more about later.

Other Late 2000s Roles

After *Doubt*, Viola was officially playing in the big leagues, and she was getting better and better roles. She played in Tom Cruise and Cameron Diaz's comedy-thriller *Knight and Day*. Later, she'd perform along with Julia Roberts in *Eat Pray Love.*

She would play Dr. Minerva in the 2010 film *It's Kind of a Funny Story.*

Viola was becoming a big name in Hollywood, and she'd star in major films like *The Help* and *Get On Up* next, two films that will be discussed in the following chapter.

Chapter 7

The Help and Get on Up

"They killed my son. He fell carrying two-by-fours at the mill. Truck run over him and crushed his lung. That white foreman threw his body on the back of a truck, drove to the colored hospital, dumped him there, and honked the horn. There was nothing they could do, so I brought my baby home. Laid him on that sofa right there. He died right in front of me. He was just 24 years old, best part of a person's life. Anniversary of his death, every year, I can't breathe, but to y'all it's just another day of bridge."

-Viola playing Aibileen in the 2011 film *The Help*

After shocking viewers and critics with her impressive acting skills in a short scene in *Doubt*, Viola was ready to take on leading lady roles in film. She did so in a powerful way in movies like *The Help* and *Get On Up*. Let us look at how these two movies shaped and grew her career.

The Help, Criticisms, and Regrets

The Help, is a period drama about an aspiring journalist, a white woman named Eugenia, who has an ongoing relationship with two black maids, Aibileen Clark and Minny Jackson. In order to establish herself as a writer and journalist, Eugenia decides to write a book about the experiences of these two women and the racism and injustice they have endured as they've worked for white families over the years. The book would be given the title that these women are often referred to as—The Help.

The movie received mostly positive reviews soon after its release in 2011, with a 76% score on Rotten Tomatoes. Some critics pointed to Viola Davis as the strongest actor in the movie, even going so far as to say that she carried the movie. As more reviews poured in, though, there was much criticism about how the movie seemed to gloss over the serious subject matter.

As for Viola personally, even though she would be nominated for an Oscar for her role in the film, she was hesitant to accept the job from the start, telling reporters, "I saw stereotype. I didn't want to put that out there."

Viola would later say that, looking back on the film, it was less about what it meant to be black, and it was more about "catering to a white audience." She'd go on to say, "The white audience at the most can sit and get an academic lesson into how we are. Then they can leave the movie theater and, hey, talk about what it meant."

"There's a part of me that feels like I betrayed myself and my people," she commented, "because I was in a movie that wasn't ready to tell the whole truth."

While *The Help* has been trashed by some for, as Viola put it, not telling the whole truth and catering to a white audience, her acting in the role has never been doubted or seen as lacking.

Get on Up—Another Minor Role that Stole the Show

In another film, Get On Up, a 2014 biopic about the singer James Brown, Viola was about to do something similar to what she did in *Doubt*— shine as a fantastic actress even though her role was not prominent in the movie.

While many reviews at the time focused on Chadwick Boseman (and for good reason),

Viola's role as James Brown's mother is unforgettable, yet another example of her shining with limited screen time, albeit this time without an Oscar nomination.

With such notable roles under her belt, Viola was poised to rise even further in her career. In the following chapter, let us look into a project that happened for Viola in two parts, ending with her getting a third Oscar nomination—and this time a win.

Chapter 8

Fences

Pittsburg in the 1950s presents itself as poor
and brown—brown buildings, rusty brown cars,
brown grass and trees—and dull, at least in this
particular neighborhood. Standing in front of one
brown house is a couple, Rose and Troy. They
are both hunched from age, and Troy's hair is
just about solid gray. They've been married for
years, but not happily so—something that is
painfully obvious from their conversation.

Troy has just admitted to his wife that he has
been having a long-term affair. In fact, the
woman he has been sleeping with is now
pregnant. In the middle of this difficult
conversation, Troy turns to talking about
baseball, a sport he played semi-professionally
in the past. Rose goes off, railing about his
bringing up a sport while he's just admitted to
cheating on his wife.

"You're not listening to me; I'm trying to explain it to you the best way I know how," Troy says. "It's not easy for me to admit that I've been standing in the same place for the past 18 years."

Rose interrupts him now, tears running down her face, her eyes bulging from anger and hurt and desperation. "I've been standing here with you. I've been right here with you, Troy. I've got a life, too. I gave 18 years of my life to stand in the spot with you!"

As Rose yells at her husband, talking about her hopes and dreams, the things she's given up to remain loyal to her husband, a man that didn't do the same for her, viewers are moved by her words and by the conviction on her face. You're hurt along with her, and you share in her outrage.

This scene, played by Denzel Washington and Viola Davis, is one of the most powerful scenes of the 2016 film *Fences*. What many viewers of this movie may not know is that both Denzel and Viola played these parts on the stage first, winning awards along the way, before bringing the same story to a wider audience by adapting it into a film.

Fences in 2013

Playwright August Wilson wrote *Fences* in 1985, a story set in the 1950s in Pittsburgh. It tells the story of a marriage between Troy and Rose Maxson, as well as Cory, a son of Rose's from a previous relationship. Troy was once a baseball player, and his love for baseball is ever-present in his dialogue. And yet, because he is a black man, his career was not as successful as he feels it should have been. Because of these disappointments, he refuses to allow his stepson, Cory, to participate in sports or accept a sports scholarship, a significant theme of the play.

It also becomes apparent early in the play that Troy is cheating on his wife. As the couple struggles economically, a friend begs Troy to break it off with his mistress, but Troy doesn't listen. When the woman becomes pregnant, Troy is forced to tell his wife about the affair. Later, the woman dies, leaving Troy with a child, whom Rose agrees to raise as her own, even though she refuses to forgive Troy for his infidelity.

Even though Troy has such a negative effect on others around him, arguably ruining the lives of both Rose and Cory, at the end of the play, when Troy has 'fought death and lost,' everyone comes together to remember the man they once loved, honoring him and choosing the see the good of his life instead of the bad things he's done.

This touching play won the 1987 Pulitzer Prize for Drama and the 1987 Tony Award for Best Play. In the late 1980s and early 1990s, the play went through several major productions.

Then, in 2010, it was put on show once again, now as a Broadway revival, this time with Denzel Washington playing Troy and Viola Davis playing Rose. A new slew of awards was given out, including the Tony Award for Best Revival of a Play. Both Denzel and Viola won the Best Performance for the show. Even though the revival was only a 13-week limited engagement, the breakout success of the play would later lead to a film adaptation starring Denzel and Viola.

The 2016 Film

Denzel Washington also produced and directed the 2016 film adaptation of *Fences*. Much praise was given by reviewers and fans for Denzel's fantastic direction and production work on the film, but Viola was also seen as a powerhouse in this role.

In fact, Viola was nominated for her third Emmy, making her the first black actress to receive three nominations. As if this were not enough, she would go on to win the Oscar for Best Actress.

While some reviews criticized the film for "feeling too much like a play" and not being cinematic enough, most reviewers praised Denzel and Viola for their acting throughout the story, further solidifying Viola's stardom.

While the film was a breakout hit, winning her an Oscar, there was another project that was taking up a great deal of her time during these same years, a project that would make Viola Davis become a household name—a little series on ABC called *How to Get Away with Murder*.

Chapter 9

How to Get Away with Murder

In movies, much work goes into introducing major characters, be they the beloved protagonist or the hated antagonist. Whether the character is a dreamy-eyed young country girl in the big city for the first time or a superhero, he or she must be presented to the viewer in a way that signals just how important they are and what kind of personality they are they have.

If a character in a movie must be introduced in a well-thought-out way, it's even more important when it comes to TV. Viewers must become attached to the main characters of a new series as quickly as possible, because it is the characters that will keep the viewers coming back much more than a nifty cliffhanger.

When Viola Davis finally decided to tackle a long-term, major TV role as Annalise Keating in *How to Get Away with Murder*, she needed to wow the viewers from the very start. People would tune back in, week after week, to see Viola play Keating. So how would the show's creators introduce Keating, a criminal defense attorney and professor of criminology? In the toughest, cockiest way possible.

"Good morning," Viola's character says as the camera follows her into the classroom, students scurrying to their places. "I don't know what terrible things you've done in your life up to this point, but clearly your karma's out of balance to get assigned to my class. I'm Professor Annalise Keating, and this is Criminal Law 100, or as I prefer to call it..." She grabs a stick of chalk and scribbles on the greenish blackboard, getting every student's attention. She turns, a self-satisfied smirk on her face, reading out what she has just written. "How to get away with murder."

The Hit Series

How to Get Away with Murder is a legal crime thriller that features a prestigious university in Philadelphia, a professor of criminal law who also actively works as a defense attorney, and how a small group of her students get her involved in a murder plot. It premiered on ABC in September of 2014 as part of their aggressive drama night-time lineup, and it aired until May of 2020. During that time, the series received massive critical acclaim and was considered a runaway hit.

The first season of the series had a lovely 85% score on Rotten Tomatoes, and many critics focused on Viola's portrayal of the main character, Professor Keating. The general consensus was that the overall storyline of the series wasn't wholly original. That said, it was well performed.

Playing Annalise Keating

Viola Davis was universally considered the star of the show, both literally and figuratively, with almost every rave review talking extensively of her acting carrying the series. As the *Los Angeles Times* wrote about *How to Get Away with Murder,* "All eyes are on Davis." This was not unexpected since she was already both a Tony winner (for the stage version of *Fences*) and an Oscar Nominee (for her small part in *Doubt*).

Watching Viola's first few minutes in the series pilot shows exactly what she brought to the character, in her hard-hitting accent, adding force and intensity to the hard and professionally cold character.

Even though, looking back, it's hard to imagine the series lasting for so many years without Viola in the lead role, as she looks back today, she talks about the scrutiny she fell under for being "too black" for the role. This, of course, plays into the concept of "colorism," which we'll discuss shortly. In addition, other black actors questioned her beauty when she was being considered for the show, saying her skin was too dark for the part.

This was not new for Viola, and she pushed passed the criticisms and racism, wowing the world with her acting skills and bringing the fantastic main character of the series to life.

Awards from the Series
After the critical reviews highlighting Viola as the heaviest hitter in the show, it's of little surprise that she was awarded the Primetime Emmy Award for Outstanding Lead Actress in a Drama Series for the role.

The series as a whole was nominated for multiple awards, winning some, such as "Television Program of the Year" from the American Film Institute, GLAAD Media's "Outstanding Drama Series," and the NAACP Image Award for "Outstanding Drama Series," and "Outstanding Actress in a Drama Series" for Viola.

It wasn't just the first season that was well received. In fact, the second season had even better reviews, featuring an impressive 93% approval rating on Rotten Tomatoes. Whenever a series manages to improve from one season to the next, that shows the tremendous potential that a group of people has to create great art. The series continued to have a loyal following through to the end, and it established Viola Davis as a household name for many American families.

Chapter 10

The First Lady

A year before *The First Lady* came out, Viola appeared on Jimmy Fallon's *The Tonight Show.* They spoke about her Oscar nomination for *Ma Rainey's Black Bottom*, as well as her then-upcoming role as Amanda Waller in *The Suicide Squad.* However, Jimmy quickly pulled the conversation toward the then-breaking news that Davis would soon be playing Michelle Obama in the series *The First Lady.* Jimmy's question: "Why would you do this? Do you have to keep testing yourself?"

Viola jokingly described it as "temporary insanity."

"The woman is a goddess," Viola explained. "Everybody knows her. Everybody wants to protect her. So I'm just going to do the best I can."

While playing the beloved First Lady was, no doubt, a high point in Viola's career, she did predict - quite accurately - how challenging the role would be. After all, fans of Michelle Obama would not be happy with anything other than the very best.

As it turned out, Viola's portrayal of Michelle Obama would take quite a bit of fire from some critics and fans alike. At the same time, though, the actress would be defended by other fans. Let us look at this series and its concept for a moment, and then we can get into the controversial role that has pushed Viola to even greater heights as an actress.

The Showtime Series

There have been many movies and series about various presidents in the history of the United States, some of the most remarkable men in history, men that have had such a profound impact on the history of humanity and the world, the direction of humanity into the future after their time as leader of the Free World, a position somewhat comparable to the Emperors of Ancient Rome. These men have so much to teach us, and the likes of Daniel Day Luis (as Lincoln) and others have brought many of those lessons to the screen.

But the wives of these presidents, arguably in one of the most influential positions in the country, having the most intimate ear of the president, the First Ladies, have amassed much less attention. That imbalance is precisely what the Showtime series *The First Lady* tries to correct.

"History hasn't focused on the women," said Cathy Schulman, one of the executive producers for the show. So they felt a challenge in honoring and revealing some of the most remarkable First Ladies in American history in a way that would be dramatic, informative, and entertaining to a modern audience.

The First Lady follows the lives of three presidents' wives, Eleanor Roosevelt, Betty Ford, and Michelle Obama, played by Gillian Anderson, Michelle Pfeiffer, and Viola Davis, respectively. Each of these actresses admitted to some trepidation when it came to playing these parts. How did Viola prepare to play the most modern of the three First Ladies in the series?

Preparing to Play the First Lady

Viola admitted that one reason she was nervous about playing Mrs. Obama was that the First Lady is such a known celebrity today. People know and love her, Viola observed, and that meant she had to work hard to get the role right. It also meant that she felt a sense of obligation to portray Michelle Obama faithfully. "I like to take artistic liberties, but I couldn't really do that here," she told reporters.

How did she prepare? She told the Wall Street Journal: "I did it all. I read every single book. I watched [the documentary] *Becoming* maybe 20 times. I stopped counting how many times I listened to her podcast. I wanted to see who she was when she was with different people."

One significant benefit Viola had was also being able to speak directly with Michelle Obama about the role, something the other actresses obviously could not do. And what did Michelle has to say to Viola? "She said, 'I'm not even an angry person.' Isn't that something?"

This left Viola with a difficult decision to make. "Listen, I am sort of an angry person, but she's not," Viola told reporters for ABC News. "And so what I wanted to do was honor her and not the perception of what Black women are supposed to be." Viola Davis is good at playing an angry woman. She brings that passion and anger from her own life to play some of the most powerful roles in her career. But she had to do something different here. She had to honor the personality that Michelle has, even if that means going against the personality Viola is most comfortable playing on the screen or stage.

Criticism

As soon as the first marketing materials for the series were released, Viola got quite a bit of backlash from a specific decision she made in playing Michelle Obama—the way she constantly pursed her lips.

To be fair, the lip pursing is something Michelle Obama does quite a bit. On top of that, as some fans pointed out the night of the premiere, "Michelle Obama appears to have an anterior open bite that Viola Davis is trying to replicate in her performance along with how she purses her lips."

Did Viola take it too far? Perhaps. Could it be the case that those that edited the series slanted the edits so that takes with the most exaggerated lip-pursing were kept in the final cut? It could be the case. Either way, while some fans and critics chose to focus entirely on that one acting choice, many are still seeing the overall work of art as something that will not be soon forgotten—and in a good way.

Chapter 11

Books, Oprah, and Future Career

Oprah Winfrey has interviewed Viola Davis in the past, and their paths have crossed from time to time. They certainly have been familiar with—and fans of—each other's work. And yet, it still came as a bit of a surprise that Oprah would elevate Viola's recent work in an even more powerful way by selecting her memoir, *Finding Me*, as an addition to her world-famous book club.

This was, indeed, a bit of a surprise precisely because Oprah rarely chooses memoirs for her book club, choosing to select works of literature (i.e., fiction) instead. But, from the first line and first paragraph, Oprah admitted, she knew this would be a book club selection.

Even some of the biggest fans of Viola's work may be surprised, though, to discover that *Finding Me* was not her first book. What other works of writing has she put out to the world? And how has *Finding Me* been received? Let us find out.

Corduroy Take a Bow

In 2018, Viola was at the top of her game in the acting world. *How to Get Away with Murder* was one of the top shows on network television, proving that the big networks can still put out high-end drama to compete with the cable networks and subscription-based streaming services. In 2017, she had been awarded the Artist of the Your Award at Harvard University. But Viola isn't satisfied with just acting. She has set her sight on something a bit different, something that involves a small stuffed bear she treasures from her childhood.

That bear is named Corduroy.

Corduroy is a book written by Don Freeman. Originally published in 1968, it follows the titular teddy bear through a department store as he searches for his lost button. Just about any American child since the 1960s has probably seen the classic red cover, simple in nature, with hardly any background at all. Instead, the cover features the bear in his green coveralls, bending over to pick up a white button, which has obviously fallen off his clothing.

Even though the book is over half a century old now, it continues to be one of the most beloved books for children. In 2007, the National Education Association launched an online poll that resulted in the book making the "Teacher's Top 100 Books for Children" list. In 2012, it was also placed in the "Top 100 Picture Books" of all time by the School Library Journal.

Since the book's original publication, it has been adapted for both film and stage multiple times. It's also become a staple for many families around the world.

In interviews, as far back as 2017, Viola talked about her plans to write a sequel for the book. "When I was five, I walked to the library by myself after school, stayed there until it got dark, and walked home." She even said that a librarian there would pack a lunch for her. That kindness made Viola feel accepted at that library, and it also kicked off her life-long love of reading.

One of young Viola's favorite books? Why, Corduroy, of course. "Corduroy has always held a special place in my life," she revealed in a press release, "first as a child paging through it, and then again with my daughter, introducing her to the adventures of that adorable teddy bear."

In March of 2018, Viola revealed the cover to her fans and followers on Twitter. Finally, in September of the same year, *Corduroy Takes a Bow* was released by Penguin Random House. It was met with fantastic success across the country, a success that was no doubt propelled by Davis fans and fans of the original Corduroy children's book.

Finding Me

In 2022, Viola added another book to her publishing name with the release of her book, *Finding Me*, a powerful, tell-all memoir. In her story, she talks about growing up poor, about her family, and about the bullying and abuse she endured from an early age. She frankly discusses the effects the words and actions had on her - and on her own sense of self-worth. But she also discusses her being able to grow beyond those things and learning that she could set ambitious goals for herself and reach them.

Also, in her book, she discusses how the series *How to Get Away with Murder* changed her life, allowing her to show a sensual, bold, and successful woman of color to a wide audience. She talks about "colorism," which involves the belief that the darker a person's skin is, the less attractive they are, less intelligent, and less valuable to others. But the concepts of colorism only hold power as long as they are believed. When they are proven false, they lose their power. They can be overcome when people, like Viola herself, stand up and show them to be ignorant falsehoods.

Finding Me has been met with critical acclaim, mainly because of the whole-hearted endorsement of several celebrities, including Oprah. Viola stated as her hope that her story will help young girls around the world—no matter the color of their skin—to see themselves with beauty and potential, just as she has learned to see herself.

Viola's Legacy Continues Beyond Books

Viola Davis has continued to work both in front of the camera and elsewhere to help those that are impoverished or pre-judged because of their race, sex, or economic situation. She spoke out as part of the Black Lives Matter movement, and she has worked tirelessly to bring new opportunities to young women of color.

Viola has gone from a starving child, a little girl that would steal food in order to survive, living in an abandoned building in which rats would keep her up at night as they killed pidgins in the walls, a young woman that was mad at the world for the injustices that were all around her, to a strong and talented actress that tries to give a voice to the voiceless, a woman who has raised millions of dollars for starving children today.

Viola's career as an actress is far from over. And her rise to stardom is not yet complete. Her books add to her message. And what does the future hold for her? You keep moving forward, and you keep making the world better for those around you. That is precisely what Viola Davis is determined to do.

Made in the USA
Columbia, SC
18 June 2022